BREAKING

THE STRONGHOLD OF

EVIL EYES

With Dangerous Prayers Against Evil Powers, Altars,
Monitoring Spirits, Eyes Of Darkness, Marine Kingdoms,
Witchcraft Altars, Ancestral Covenants, Spells And Curses

APOSTLE E.N. LIVINUS

TABLE OF CONTENTS

INTRODUCTIONS

In this life there are numerous vice, many things, evils that happens in the dark. People, human beings are being terrorized on daily bases by powers of darkness, spiritual wickedness in high places without them knowing the source of there problems; the devil in his evil agenda carry out evil works against them to ensure they are enslaved throughout their life time.

Do you know what makes nations rise against nation? Do you know why men fall sick or why there are epidemic monitors, and people die like fowls, that is evil eyes that is evil eyes that monitors the affairs of men.

Those evil eyes checkmates activities of men, and either block their goals or kill them entirely. Remember, the evil eyes are always from the devil, he is always on his mission, to steal, kill, and to destroy destinies and lives.

So he always set a device to be able to champion his infernal activities which is always dangerous to the joy and sweet survival of man.

However, God has not ever denied or hidden from His creatures, He had made a way for deliverance to shows His loving kindness to as many that would turn to Him for deliverance from their troubles.

In this book, you will be privileged to see issues concerning those evil monitors, who they are, what they do, their trick of operations, their victims, what and how to do so as to escape their control and evils, and many more ways for spiritual warfare and deliverance.

Get this book, and read and practice diligently all the counsels in order, for your complete deliverance and maintenance of a continuous freedom all through your life time. And also have assurance of eternal life, a life without pains, secured in Heaven for you in Jesus name.

Spiritual warfare are battles in the spiritual realm, though fought in the spiritual realm but need to be prepared physically, knowing what you are doing and what spiritual weapon and armors to put in use for maximum successful results.

A mistake or negligence of any piece of spiritual weapon or armor makes you disqualified and unfit for smooth and victorious manifestations. So, you have to be careful because whatever a man sows he will also reap at the process of time.

If you can show faith and be diligent to observe and to do according to all the counsels of this book which is according to biblical directives, you will not only eat the fruit of the land, but you will be blessed, and also be a blessing to as many that comes your way.

Information brings formations and deliverance, as you have the grace to discover this book, buy it and carefully follow the rules to get yourself freed from the menace of evil monitors, and get for your family and friends to ensure an all round deliverance in your life by the grace of God. You are blessed.

CHAPTER ONE

WHAT IS EVIL MONITORS

You can see as the name sounds; "evil". In this life there is always two significance and outstanding powers that governs the affairs of men; and that is the good, and the evil or bad powers.

There is no man that can stand at the fence; it is either you are standing at the good or you give in to the control of the evil. All these two foundations are under the control of spirits; bad or evil spirits, and good or Holy spirit; one from the Lord God our creator, and the other from the devil, and evil spirit.

In Psalm 104:4; we read that God made His Angels Spirits and His ministers a flame of fire. This acts of God was for the smooth performance of His purpose on His creatures here on earth. His minister's device means to carry out their assignments to the glory of their master, the king of kings.

The devil is an old man (old serpent) Revelation 20:2; He laid hold of the dragon, that serpent of old, who is the devil and Satan..., he is wiser than man, and would always want to measure rank with God, but he is a deceiver and a looser. In his plans, he always think faster than man to make sure that he pull him down into captivity, hence he set out watchers, unseen evil eyes that monitors men and their affairs.

2 Corinthians 11:12-15 but what I do, I will also continue to do, that I may cut off the opportunity from those who desire an opportunity to be regarded just as we are in the things which they boast. For such are false apostles, deceitful workers, transforming themselves into apostles of Christ.

And no wonder! For satan himself transforms himself into an angel of light. Therefore it is no great thing if his ministers transforms also transforms themselves into ministers of righteousness, whose end will be according to their works

This means that there are evil eyes monitoring you; they are spiritual wickedness in high places; though they use men to some reasonable extent. They have been assigned to police you day and night, any where you go; sleeping or awake, eating or drinking, while happy with friends or annoyed with oppositions; they are always there closer than you can imagine to destroy you and your plans.

However, the purpose of this book is not to terrify or frighten you over the fact of the existence of the plans and agents of the devil in and around you, but to expose them to your nearest understanding, to highlight their activities, and to reveal to you the possible ways you can raise up a battle cry against them and win them out rightly in battle.

THEIR AGENTS

Evil monitors though spiritual eyes, but works through men with Satanic spiritual back up. The devil influence those his human agents with his evil spirit to carry out evil acts or assignment. They as were filled with evil powers, were made able to watch and view and manipulate activities of the people without them knowing until the person concern either sin or make mistake, then they will finally appear to harm or to dominate so as to terminate the work of God in his life.

Those agents, as were filled with the spirit of Satan has developed satanic characters; they are now hatters of good things, and lovers of evil activities that would make their master glad, and gain approval for them from their master, the devil.

Their heart have been over turned to do only what that pleases their master; they have been programmed in their heart to do evil and enjoy it as sports not minding what ails who or who is crying or dying; they have been commissioned to do evil, and they have equipments to carry out their duties fixed in their system. They uses the following people or group of persons as agents.

1.PRESIDENTS/ KINGS

Some kings are evil, and as such are usually not happy seeing other kings or nations prosper or be in peace. Anytime they took notice of a prosperous king or nation, they will go to impose war to devastate them and frustrate their peace.

Even when they are not good or strong enough, they seek for external forces to support them, only to make sure that they commit evil to please their master. You can see what that happened in the book of second kings, that was an example of evil monitors; evil eyes watching to do evil to whoever they target.

2 Chronicles 20:1; it happen after this that the people of Moab with the people of Ammon, and others with them besides the Ammonites, came to battle against Jehoshaphat.

Jehoshaphat was the king of Judah who fears God, and was working to build his kingdom in the fear of God. Reading from chapter nineteen verse four to seven; and he advised the judges to deal with the people in the fear of God.

While he was busy building his territory, he never know that evil eyes were watching and monitoring all his activities until too late; when they have organized and was ready to fight him.

This evil people imposes evil even to the whole world to make sure that the people suffer or even die; when people die any how, they rejoice, they love seeing blood of men wasted for no reason.

1 King21:13; and two men, scoundrels, came in and sat before him, and the scoundrels witnessed against him, against Naboth, in the presence of the people, saying, Naboth has blasphemed God and the king! Then they took him outside the city and stoned him with stones, so that he died.

Take for instance when there was covid19 and other epidemics; that was the menace of evil monitors. They sponsored the wastage of lives all over the world, and they are happy to perform their evil duties.

1 Kings 21:16; so it was, when Ahab heard that Naboth was dead, that Ahab got up and went down to take possession of the vineyard of Naboth the Jezreelite.

But as I said earlier, this book is not to frighten or make you feel unsafe, but to let you know that God is able to save you in whatever troubles you found yourself.

Exodus 14:14; the Lord will fight for you and you shall hold your peace.

Now, because Jehoshaphat fears the Lord, he quickly devised a means to tackle the situation in the name of the Lord through prayers, and God gave him His helping hands, and delivered him.

PRAYERS

1. O Lord my God, in you I put my trust, have mercy on me and show me your kindness, and deliver me from evil monitors, and their evil agendas in Jesus name.

2. My hope is on you O Lord, I will live my life for you, walking in the light of your word all the days of my life in Jesus name.

3. I cover my life and my territory with the blood of Jesus, and I frustrate every monitoring eye of the powers of darkness against my life in Jesus name.

4. I refuse to fall into the hands of my enemies, therefore I command every evil ground of my enemies to break, and let all their plans be scattered in Jesus name.

5. O Lord my king, your word is a lamp to my feet, and a light to my feet; guide me in the light of your words that I may be able to stand against the wiles of my enemies in Jesus name.

2.MARMAID SPIRITS

This is usually said to be spirits operating through the water regions, but they causes destructions to sons of men whose heart are porous for them to enter, and perform their commission.

Usually this spirit enters into humans as they monitor their victims, but they cannot attack an individual unless he open way for them by allowing sin in his life. Sins opens way for the devil to operate and display his evil works.

Marmaid spirits monitors young folks, and even older ones to steal their glory and hinder them from becoming what God destined them to be in life by leading them into murder and sins of fornication.

You actually may not know what they were doing until they trap you down into sin of immorality or murder, and then come in to destroy your life; they present love and high life, but they are wolfs in sheep clothing ready to destroy without mercy.

Matthew 7:15; beware of false prophets, who comes in to you in sheep's clothing, but inwardly they are ravenous wolves.

They act friendly in disguise to what they have at the back of their mind; they present love, enjoyment and power, where as they have poisonous venom in their teeth. Immediately as they bite, their poison will travel down your system, and to your brain and may cause death.

That happened to the great and anointed man called Samson. He was anointed by God from birth, and the Spirit of God comes upon him at intervals to use him for some wonderful works; at one occasion he killed lion with his bare hands, he killed many Philistines with ordinary jaw bone; he was just doing mighty works but he did not know that evil eyes were watching him; they monitored his activities, what he likes and what he likes doing until they trapped him down with a woman; he loves women, what a tragedy.

Judges 16;1; now Samson went to Gaza and saw a harlot there, and went in to her.

The issue concerning strange women opened up a channel for his destruction; the spirit in charge rued him to a very dangerous agent of the devil, the daughter of Jezebel named Delilah in verse four of Judges chapter 16.

Delilah presented fake love to Samson, but conspired with the enemies of Samson, who was also called the strong man. Samson was strong man indeed, but the source of his strength was not man made but divine; so the evil watchers saw him, and pressed to destroy him with what he loves doing. They disconnected him firstly from his God.

He played with his source of power and glory, and defiled himself; immediately the Spirit of God left him, and he became like ordinary men, then they laid hands on him and plucked out his two eyes. Imagine how the once called strong man was destroyed; "evil monitor".

What about the wisest man on earth, king Solomon? He loved the Lord so much that at one time he scarified a thousand burnt offerings to the Lord. The Lord loved him also and gave him wisdom and riches.

But Solomon later turned to love many women. 1 Kings 11:1-2; but king Solomon loved many foreign women, as well as the daughters of Pharaoh; women of the Moabites, Ammonites, Edomites, Sidonians, and Hitttites-

from the nations of whom the Lord had said to the children of Israel, you shall not intermarry with them, nor they with you. Surely they will turn away your hearts after their gods. Solomon clung to these in love.

Don't you know that there are unseen eyes that are watching you? Be careful where you go and how you behave; they want to rue you into sin, and ruin your life, be warned.

PRAYER

1. I will not die in the hands of my enemy, help me Lord and lead me in the path of righteousness in Jesus name.

2. Into your saving hands I commit my life, both spirit, soul and body; deliver me O Lord from all the traps and schemes of my enemy and destroyers in Jesus name.

3. I refuse to play with weapons that will take my life, O God my Father, let your unseen hands protect me from every evil hands stretched to capture me in Jesus name.

4. O God My Lord, give me the grace to know you more and more, studying your words every day, and meditating in your laws every day in Jesus name.

5. I open the door of my heart for the Spirit of grace, Come Holy Spirit and fill my heart with the joy of the Lord, and kindle in me the fire of the Lord in Jesus name.

3.MEDIUM/WITCH DOCTORS

Though the devil have been committing different types of evil in and around the whole world, yet, the devil has not appeared physically to carry anyone into sin or rued anyone into disobedient to the laws of God.

What the devil does is tricks, he deceives men into acts that leads them away from the covering and protections of God. As the devil trick you into sin, the Spirit of God that also watches over you will turn away from you, leaving you to the mercy of the devil, and you know that there is nothing like that; the devil cannot show you mercy.

People who visit Medium or witch doctors have defiled themselves, and are no longer under the protective hands of the almighty God or His Spirits. You may think that it is just a mere visit, you might not know that you are under the control of powers of darkness, as they have been monitoring to push you out of the grace and protections of God.

Leviticus 19:31; give no regards to mediums and familiar spirits; do not seek after them, to be defiled by them, I am the Lord your God.

Your God is able to protect you in all circumstances, do not go to make charm for your protections or to inquire from their hands, they are traps, destructive pits that are ready to swallow whoever that falls inside.

Ephesians 6:11; put on the whole armor of God, that you may be able to stand against the wiles of the devil.

The devil has no power over the saints of God, he can only use his tricks, but when you have fortified yourself with the armor of the truth and the sword of the spirit which is the word of God; he will not penetrate or be able to harm you at all in Jesus name.

PRAYERS

1. I cover my life and family with the blood of Jesus, and I submit my life to the control of the Holy Spirit in Jesus name.

2. I decree and declare; I will never bow my head to the devil nor go to inquire in his house in Jesus name.

3. I rededicate my life unto God, to live and obey Him all the days of my life, and to inquire in His house in Jesus name.

4. The glory of the Lord is all over me, I will not walk in the counsel of the ungodly or sit on the seat of sinners to open doors for the devil against my life in Jesus name.

5. I will live for Jesus day after day, and I vow to obey the Holy Spirit, and to walk as He leads me on this planet earth in Jesus name.

4.FAMILIAR SPIRITS

God is Spirit but He uses men as an instrument to navigate His works and purposes here on earth. There are many works in the mind of God to carry out or reach out to every creature, examples, preaching the gospels, and delivering them that were oppressed by the devil through the gospel, and the declarations of the word of faith.

God is at work to perfect all those plans of His heart, but He uses men to carry them out, and they are moving successfully, so He backed men up by His Spirit to do what only God can do in the life of men.

In the same way, the devil has numerous programs through which he catch up with men; which includes bringing into captivity all men so that they will be victims of death and hell fire through sin.

 And to achieve his plans, he goes about using some falling spirits that operates near you; they knows you, what you like and what you dislike.

Those familiar spirits goes round about your life, presenting some desires that you are used to which does not give glory to God. And you never know that they are waiting for the day that you will fall into any of them, and the devil will strike you at a bad junction which you may not be able to overcome.

To stay victorious over this agent of the devil you must deep yourself into serious studies of the word of God; reading to observe and to do all that He commanded, this will go a long way to correct your way to the fear of God and Holy living which is the high way to overcome powers of darkness.

It is only holy living that will make someone to escape the evil of familiar spirit and to overcome them promptly.

PRAYERS

1. I cry unto you my dear God, many are the tricks of my enemies against me, but you will deliver me from all of them in Jesus name.

2. Your Spirit gives me insight on how to do and what to do, O Lord my king, do not cast me away

from your presence or take your Spirit away from me in Jesus name.

3. I delight my life in your love, your love connect me to your grace and transferred me into the kingdom of your dear Son Jesus; keep me O Lord in You love in Jesus name.

4. I cover my spirit soul and body with the blood of Jesus, and I break every link of familiar spirit to my life in Jesus name.

5. Your right hands O Lord does valiantly, let you hands destroy every spirit contending against my safety in Jesus name.

MODE OF OPERATIONS.

Evil monitors are evil as their name sounds, and they use evil and diabolic means to carry out their evil acts of monitoring to see who and how to fight or injure their victim.

Some of the ways they use to fight or monitor are as follows:

1.EVIL ALTARS

People do not know what altars stands for, that is why they joke or play about when it comes up to either break or raise one for themselves. Altar is a place of fellowship with spirits, place of judgment, and it can either be with good spirit or bad one as the case may be.

But whichever way, the spirit that was consciously or unconsciously gathered in an altar monitors the person on whose behalf they gather; if it is a good spirit, they will monitor to protect and guide him wherever he goes.

But the negative spirit will only prove his name, and perform his duties according to his origin and assignment which is to steal, kill and destroy. Evil altars have been a barrier to many who was once their patronizers but later changed to going to church without being rooted to the things of God.

Not rooted in the things of God means that they are still living a double faced life; life of hypocrites, going to church but living in sin. This type of person will find it difficult to escape the destructions done to men by evil monitors because they have no covering or defense.

The Spirit of God is ever ready to save and to deliver whoever that runs to Christ in true repentance, but will not account for sinners and people that joke with the laws and counsels of God.

People in this shoes will suffer damages as unbelievers because they are not known or registered in the Lamb book of life; they will not partake in the divine protections that God gives to his chosen..

PRAYERS

1.I declare in the name of Jesus Christ, I belong to Jesus, I dedicate my life and my entire worship to the almighty God, I will never go back to sin and satan again in Jesus name.

2. I refuse to bow my head to any other God, I belong to Jesus Christ and Him alone.

3. O Lord unto your care I commit my life and all my affairs, keep me in all my ways, and make my works prosperous in Jesus name.

4. I renounce every enchantment and divination/ sacrifice that was made over my head in Jesus name.

5. I stand upon the word of God, and the power in the blood of Jesus, and I revoke every agreement and oath I entered with any spirit or idols in Jesus name.

2.EVIL MIRROR

Evil monitors sees people they are monitoring completely wherever they go, hence they are always able to track them and do whatever they want with them because they are stronger than their victims since they operate with spiritual back up.

With the aid of their mirror which is not ordinary, they control their victim, their distance not withstanding. Even if you go across the sea, they still monitors and carry out their evil plans.

Their victims will be experiencing set backs, manipulations, but would not know what was happening to them. Some would go to witch doctors to inquire as they don't know the scripture; they don't know that they are worsening their situations.

Many people died in the torment because they don't know what was wrong with them, neither can they think of going or praying for deliverance because they don't know the scripture, or the way to God for help.

PRAYERS

1.I hide myself under the covering of the blood of Jesus, I will not be manipulated by agents of darkness in Jesus name.

2. I submit my life into the power of the almighty God, I refuse the agendas of evil manipulators in Jesus name.

3. I cover my destiny with the blood of Jesus, O God, let your glory cover me so that I will be safe from all the evils of evil eyes in Jesus name.

4. My life is hidden in Jesus Christ, and in God, I am not a candidate to the devil, and he can do me no harm in Jesus name.

5. Favor and blessings of God is my portions, I am delivered from evil manipulators in Jesus name.

3.BOWL OF WATER

Water reflects just like mirror, evil monitors use the reflections to manipulate and attract their victims. When they make incantations, armed with some fetish material, their victims will appear inside the bowl of water in front of the agents that are using the means to manipulate him.

But the victim will not know, the agent of darkness can cause harm; either kill or maim the victim or blind his eyes. He can do any thing he wants to him because he is standing right inside the bowl before him helplessly.

It is a dangerous experience, that is how some people suddenly develop pains in their eyes, stomach or in any part of his body, and some even die mysteriously as they kill them in that bowl.

There are yet more means the evil monitors work to harm their victim; some use rings, talisman or charm they hang or tie round their waist. People under the torment and control of evil monitors and sees all there victims wherever he may be.

PRAYERS

1.The Spirit of the Lord God is upon me, and He has given me sound mind, I will not be brought under the control of powers of darkness in Jesus name.

2. I was bought by the precious blood of Jesus, and I am free from every blood contaminations that could bring me under bondage in Jesus name.

3. As I pray in the name of Jesus every knee bows before me because I am in authority in the name of Jesus name.

4. I am free from every generational curse, for the blood of Jesus Christ has set me free from every evil blood, and I am free in Jesus name.

5. I am found in Christ, I have a divine origin, therefore I will not be under bondage of powers of darkness in Jesus name.

CHAPTER TWO

THEIR TARGETS

The devil is as his name sounds; evil. He does not do good or associate with any move that will fetch anything good to anyone. He is the enemy of all, both the white and the Negro, he does not spare anybody; both people that do good and people that are ignorant of his existence and his evil works on his loyal; people under his control. So every body need to be careful, stay awake and be at watch to avoid being a victim of his devices.

1 Peter 5:8; be sober, be vigilant; because your adversary the devil walks about like a roaring lion, seeking whom he may devour.

The devil has set up his device in the spiritual realm, he has stretched out his arms towards all the earth and all that are living in it to perform his duties which includes; stealing, to kill, and to destroy.

He does not spare rather he kills to the point of total annihilation unless some thing serious was done to save the situation. He does not show pity or consider a consultation to bribe him; he stops at nothing unless the attentions of a higher order of the almighty power of the living God was consulted to end the destructive power of his agents.

Evil monitors targets every thing that is good; human beings, animals and things to turn them into disorder or against their wishes. They monitor national health and economy to make sure that the people suffer or be in agony.

We will discuss few out of their numerous target just to draw out the picture of what I am talking about.

1.NATIONS.

When we talk about nations, we are talking at a large extent about people that are living in that nation, the nationals. If a country is at peace, the people rejoice; but when things go bad in a country every body mourn.

Things that makes a nation or country happy includes, good security, peace, good economy, which is the hand work of good governance. But when any of these things are not in order, the people suffer, and evil will abound in the land.

Evil eye that monitors from a distance to cripple nations and ensure pain and poverty just to manifest their wicked missions as assigned by the devil.

The devil is always on the lookout to attacking peaceful nations just to wipe away peace, and drink their economy as water. A nation at peace may not know that there are unseen eyes that are watching to see what to do so as to cause confusion or war. You know, when war comes in, the economy will fall; there will be no security, and the people will be in trouble as there will be no security or a cool headed person to control the citizens.

As evil eye or evil watchers are targeting nations, they are aiming at kings too. A king may think that he has gotten to the end of the world, or he is now the man on top, and he start behaving as he likes; the evil watchers will just throw one arrow, and destabilize his system, and that ends it all.

That is why you hear that a president slept and could not wake or that he made one none sense statement or decree, and the nation got on fire; that is the work of evil eye; evil watcher. Be careful of evil eyes, they are watching from a distance, and they are close to catch up with you if you loose guard or walk in unrighteousness.

Anytime the evil watchers discovers that the nation is living in iniquity, they will bounce on the country, and must achieve their proposed evil as there will be no power to hinder them.

Sin opens way for evil watchers to come in, when they come in, it will take the grace of God for the nation to be restored or healed. Your nation will not be under the attack of evil monitors in Jesus name.

Ahab was a wicked king, his wife, Jezebel was a wicked queen who sponsors killings and all sorts of wickedness. Evil eye spotted the nation, Samaria;

and Syrian army blocked their way, ready to come in and destroy them. Their gate was shut, no body was going in and no one was coming out, and famine dealt with them; 2 Kings6:24.

Both the king and commoners were down with hunger, and it was a serious case, but it took the intervention of prophet Elisha to prophesy over the land before God restore peace, put the Syrian soldiers to flight, and restore abundance to the land again 2 Kings Ch. 7.

Proverbs 14:34; righteousness exalts a nation, but sin is a reproach to any people.

PRAYERS

1. Have mercy on me O Lord, and deliver me an d my nation from the hands of evil watchers in Jesus name.

2. I confess Jesus Christ as my Lord and Savior, and I dedicate my entire family to God; to worship, and to serve in Jesus name.

3. I confess before men and all my brethren that I have chosen the way of Jesus, and I am begging God

to spare my life, and not to destroy me with the wicked in Jesus name.

4. I refuse to be destroyed with the wicked, so I live my life for Jesus for onward protection in all areas of life in Jesus name.

5. I cover my nation and my entire house hold with the blood of Jesus, we shall not be exposed to the evil ones in Jesus name.

2. FAMILY

Family can be immediate, extended or both, whichever way, in as much as you are a member of the family, you have the same blood connection, and you are to a larger percentage united to gain or to loose in spiritual realm.

Whatever one does connect to all in the spiritual realm, unless where there is a separation by divine order. To be separated by divine order means being involved in a God driven motion, call or order or a belief that brings salvations.

Romans 8:1; there is now no condemnation to those who are in Christ Jesus, who do not walk according to the flesh, but according to the Spirit.

The only thing that can separate a man from the evil or miss appropriations and sins of his family is when a man give his life to Jesus, and continue his life with the fear of God.

At this point, the Holy Spirit comes into his heart, and regenerates his entire being into the person of Jesus Christ; the word of God will at this point be a light unto his paths; guiding and protecting in all his ways.

The blood of Jesus Christ would have washed him clean from all sins, and set him free from known and unknown sins; He will be born again.

On this ground, the evil of the fathers will not be traceable to him; this is because he is now a new creature; born in the image and likeness of the father above, and not his earthly fathers.

Otherwise, it will interest you to know that evil eyes are watching every family, and are getting ready to punish any and everyone that would open the door for them through sins or indulgence in any evil character.

Usually, the evil eyes or the evil watcher do impose curses or spiritual embargo on any ailing family as a punishment on disobedient. That is why some people suffer late marriage, divorce, untimely death etc as a family curse, and every member suffers it until Christ comes in to deliver.

Families have been a long time target for evil eyes because many people are involved. It is through family that a nation springs up, and having a family in cage is like an access towards getting the whole nation into bondage.

Families are very prone to evil captivity because all members do not live together or come up at the same time; they live from generation to generation. Some generations are purely ignorant of the laws of God; hence they lived in total disobedient to the laws of God, and some who knows does not care.

While some families does not even know what their fathers committed before they were born, so they came up and start living as if all things are well; this is dangerous, but to be on a safe side, all should surrender to Jesus Christ for safety and a complete deliverance from all evil influence.

PRAYER

1. I decree, and declare that I belong to Jesus, and I dedicate my life to Him in Jesus name.

2. The blood of Jesus cleanses me from every blood contamination, and I am free from every evil works in Jesus name.

3. Jesus Christ has carried away curses from my family because He died on the cross for my sake; I am free in Jesus name.

4. I am wiser than my enemies because I know the word of God; therefore I have escaped the tricks of the devil in Jesus name.

5. I will never give room for the agents of the devil to harm my family, and I exempt my self from the evil of my father's house in Jesus name.

3. MARRIAGES

Marriage is a divine institution; it was God that originated it, and He stated what it is and how it should be carried out, and how it should not be conducted. Failure to go into marriage or conduct it in a good and God way attracts curse from God, and opens way for the evil monitor to let in evil omen into marriage.

Many men and women goes into marriage without taking thought of the laws of God concerning marriage. They just jump into living with a woman at there own time and their own style; it is evil in the sight of God.

Marriage should be kept holy, not just to please God and receive His blessings; but to avoid the evil of these watchers. The evil eye is watching to see you make mistake or offend God so that as the Spirit of God that is watching over you turns away, they will strike and gain advantage over your life.

Hebrew 13:4; marriage is honorable among all, and the bed undefiled; but fornications and adulterers God will judge.

It an agony of the highest orders for people to be living in a perpetual fornication and call themselves husband and wife; it is an error that needs urgent correction. You are a fornicator when you are living with a woman that is not lawfully married to you.

You better change now and seek for forgiveness, so that God will forgive you and deliver you from the hands of evil monitors who has already crept into your life because of your errors.

PRAYERS

1.Have mercy on me O Lord according to your loving kindness, and deliver me from my errors, and the wickedness of evil eyes that are watching to destroy my life.

2. I repent today of every mistake in my marriage, and I cry out for deliverance from the destructions of the evil monitors in Jesus name.

3. I will make my life the dwelling place of the most High, and I will build His throne in my heart to worship and adore Him in Jesus name.

4. I shield my life with the blood of Jesus Christ, and I destroy every evil release from the kingdom of darkness into my life in Jesus name.

5. Spirit of the Living God, please come afresh on me, and raise me up to your standard, a level where the devil can never be able to touch or harm me in Jesus name.

4. BUSINESSES

Business can be defined as a process where we buy and sell goods and services or our effort to make ends met. In the process of buying goods and services, some people are independent or sole business owners, while some are in partnership; other groups are in the sell of services or provisions of services, employers, working in another man's office.

Which ever way, it can be summed up to be under the umbrella of stewardship, and the word of God has standards for stewardships

1 Corinthians 4:2; moreover it is required in stewardship that one be found faithful.

Faithfulness means rendering the agreed services in sincerity; without deceit or lies. This goes a long way to mean that as you are sell your goods, you will be truthful concerning all that you do, the measurements, the mixtures, the components and all that connects to what you are selling must be done in a right way.

In the other way, as you render services, be sincere, go to your office on time, and give truthful report and service as agreed with your clients or your boss. It is quite tempting as human beings are selfish, and always looking for gain at the high side, but God wants you to be honest so you can remain under His protective grace.

In all, you must be found faithful. The danger in all these things is that the evil monitor is watching very close, and seeing everything you do whether in the open or in the secret to see if you will make mistake or be in offense.

Not ready to pay you in the area you get things right, but very much ready to strike you immediately you fall into offense.

You must be very careful in your business, whether buying, selling or rendering services because you are the target of evil monitors to use and display their wickedness. You must be extra careful, the devil is looking for someone to devour.

PRAYER

1.My life is hidden in Christ, I have made up my mind, I will live for Jesus every day and every moment in Jesus name.

2. O Lord my Father, your grace is ever sufficient for me, I cannot do it all alone; I need you every day Lord in Jesus name.

3. I stand and I plead the blood of Jesus against every trick of the devil to rue me into unfaithfulness, I withstand them all in Jesus name.

4. I will never let the devil win the battle, neither will I compromise with sin no matter their troubles in Jesus name.

5. Come O Holy Spirit and always shine the light of the Lord into my heart through the word of God so I can be fortified to will all the time in Jesus name.

5.MINISTRY

There should be a wide and good understanding about ministry; what it means and how to carry it out. Inability to full understanding of ministry makes many to go into error but still thinks that they are serving the Lord.

Ministry is not to be served or worshiped; it is not wearing a coat of sinlessness or a garment of righteousness. Rather, ministry is all about service; stewardship. You are gathering people to serve them and not to be served. You need to be corrected.

Again, in ministry, it is what you are given that you deliver; you cannot give what you don't have. When you want to give or serve what you don't have you will be pushed into error, there is no competition in destiny, manage what you have, and more may be given to you if you do well.

Remember, the evil monitor is watching to put a yoke on you whenever he sees you misbehave or go astray.

Are you a teacher in your ministry? Remain a teacher, and don't try to prophesy or to give prophecy. Are you an evangelist? Maintain your calling and your gift. But if you desire to prophesy or to teach like a gifted teacher; you go back to God in prayers. It is God that gives gifts; you don't fake the gift of God, it is an error, you are looking for His wrath, repent, and He will beautify you.

Remember the evil eye is watching you; don't fake the gift of God, it is an offense and sin against the Holy Spirit.

PRAYER

1.I have chosen the way of Jesus Christ, I will neither turn left nor right, O God make your grace available for me in Jesus name.

2. O God my Father, uphold me to the end so I will not start well and end in disaster in Jesus name.

3. Let your hands on me manifest greatness, wisdom, sound mind and excellence performance, so I can do your work with boldness in Jesus name.

4. My lips shall praise you Lord, thus will I bless you in all my endeavors, reveal yourself more and more to me in Jesus name.

5. I cover my ministry, my calling and election, and I commit my life unto your able hands Lord; be my dwelling place in Jesus name.

6.PERSONALITY/ INDIVIDUALS

The evil monitor does not respect any body; mister president, his cabinets, and the lowest person if anything like that, are all in his list of target, he is looking for all. Just like the call of God for repentance is for all, the devil wants every body to enter his trap and be under bondage.

 He is actually not looking for your color but for your soul to destroy. A wise person; that is people that are in Christ doesn't give the devil a chance because they know his tricks; he is a thief.

John 10:10; the thief does not come except to steal, and to kill, and to destroy. I have come that they may have life, and that they may have it more abundantly.

It is a foolish thought to think that the evil monitor does not see you, either because you are too holy, you are too big or rich, or because you are no body in the society.

The evil monitor is an agent assigned to capture all men to satan, That was why he stretched out his wide dish of monitoring eyes to scan even through the darkness, walls and mountains.

But, there is escape in God through Jesus Christ; not that he will not see you, but he can do you no harm; that is because there is no sin in you, and the glory of God covers you wherever you go; the evil monitor have nothing in you.

PRAYER

1. My life is hidden in God through Jesus Christ, the evil monitor has nothing in me in Jesus name.

2. I will live my life to please my God, my maker, and I know He will not allow my feet to be moved.

3. I have made up my mind to honor and obey the voice of the Holy Spirit, He will guide me in all my ways in Jesus name.

4. O my God, give me power everyday, my strength is not enough, I need you all the time Lord in JESUS NAME.

5. I cover my faith and my confessions with the blood of Jesus, and I frustrate the powers of evil monitors over my life in Jesus name.

CHAPTER THREE

SIGNS OF EVIL MONITORS

---

1 John 5:19; we know that we are of God, and the whole world lies under the away of the wicked one.

Since the devil was dethroned from heaven, and cast down into the world, the world has been in trouble. Powers of darkness have not rested where they were fighting to win men into their kingdom against the wishes of God.

It is no longer a hidden story; the devil has spread his evil net wide with every effort to capture all men, even the elect of God. But that is even why Jesus Christ was manifested, so He can destroy all the works of the devil and his agents.

The savior from the evils of the devil and his cohorts can only come throw pursuit of God through His words. The knowledge of the laws of God brings wisdom which is very vital for human deliverance and blessings.

Proverbs 6:23; for the commandment is a lamp, and the law is a light; reproofs of instruction are the way of life.

Your prosperity can only be complete when you have given your life totally to the study of the words and commands of God; His word will introduce a life that will shine as light in all your ways.

Which means that you will not be in darkness or ignorant of what is happening in this life; whether physically or spiritually; His Spirit will teach you all things.

Long time before now, human beings did not know some tricks of the devil until they turn, and give their lives to Jesus Christ. This single move gave birth to the in coming of the Holy Spirit who reveals all things

If you have not given your life to Jesus Christ, you will not receive the gift of the Holy Spirit who will in turn reveal things to you. As the Holy Spirit is not yet in your life, you will be in darkness, and ignorant, you will not know spiritual matters, and you will be captured by your enemy, the devil.

Deuteronomy 29:29; the secret things belongs to the Lord our God, but those things which are revealed belong to us and our children forever, that we may do the words of this law.

So by the revelations of the Lord our God through the help of the Holy Spirit, we were made to know about signs of evil monitors and other strategies of the devils. As we continue, we will be revealing them from step to step.

1.WHEN YOU DISCOVER A PARTICULAR ANIMAL ALWAYS AROUND YOU.

Evil monitors are spirit beings, but they often use some animals to carry out their works. Some times they will be using Lizards, Rats, dogs, snake, Birds, Cockroaches, wall gecko etc to carry out their monitoring assignments.

With this at work, you will often be seeing them around you, following you up but physically and even in your dreams. Sometimes, you will be seeing them with your inner eyes even while you are awake; you will be seeing them while someone with you may not be seeing them the way you do.

Any time you start noticing such movements in and around you, you have to stay awake spiritually to fight in a spiritual warfare because they are in to destroy some vital virtues in and around you.

2. WHEN YOU START FEELING THE PRESENCE OF SOMEONE AROUND YOU.

The glory and the blessings of God in and around us comes to us spiritually before manifestation into the physical. You may not see them because they are spiritually released by God.

So, the devil has now devised to pose a hindrance in the spiritual realm also to stop any good thing coming your way from the table of the Almighty. So he set up some spiritual beings to keep hovering around you, and to divert your God approved blessings.

Any time you sense such movement around you, even though you are not seeing or touching them, it will pay you well to consult heaven for a fight over your inheritance.

You will be delivered, but you have to follow some guide line for spiritual warfare which will attract some Host of heaven to assist and set you free.

3. WHEN YOU NOTICE THAT YOU ARE MOVING UP AND DOWN

The devil in the name of Jesus have no power, but he uses tricks to deceive his victims into pits that will help him bind them up. He gains access into your life because of sinfulness he found in you, so he now come and gain ground to manipulate your efforts.

If there is no sin in your life, the devil will not be able to come into your life or take or hinder what that belong to you. Spirit beings, powers of darkness are always in charge of failures, and are looking for sins in your life so they can gain access.

They will not allow you to rest or to move forward in life; your life will be a sample of rising and falling. When you notice such, be aware that the enemies of your life are at war against your prosperity.

However, you can resist them through prayers, warfare prayers to quench their fire over your life.

4. FAILURE AT THE EDGE OF BREAKTHROUGH

Evil monitors are always watching to see and divert good things away from your life. Prayerful Christians are always awake to stand against them ; but when one is not praying, the evil monitor will have a wide room to display his evil omens in his life.

So, when you notice that things are not moving the way you wanted them, when you discover that there is a near success syndrome. You always fail at the edge of your breakthrough; there is danger, get ready to pray; evil monitors are at work against you.

5. WHEN YOUR BELONGINGS BEGAN TO MISS MYSTERIOUSLY

This dangerous spirits always like to lay hands on something that they will use to manipulate your life. It may be your shoes, cloths etc. They mysteriously seize any of those things to their covens to use against you.

To some people, they may not take it serious; they may take is as a light thing. But it is a serious matter that should be given time and attention to seek after, and to back up your search with serious warfare prayers.

So, don't give the devil a chance, resist him seriously in your prayers. The devil you fail to fight and resist today will rise to stop you tomorrow. They are witchcrafts, and you don't allow a witch to live, kill him immediately.

6. WHEN YOU START HEARING YOUR NAME ESPECIALLY IN THE NIGHT.

Evil watchers are always at alert to perform their evil works. As spiritual beings, they can use anything, and can pass through any barrier, and can use any strategy to attract your attention.

If you hear people call your name especially in the night, don't answer unless you are sure of the person calling you. If you answer their call, they will gain ground over your life; although that is for people that are not under spiritual security by the blood of Jesus.

If you are born again, they will not get you or use that trick to come against you, but they may use some other means which will require serious prayers to fight them back to get your freedom. So be wise, and wake up to pray.

7. WHEN YOU SEE BLOOD STAIN AT YOUR DOOR POST

Blood has since creation been a strong weapon for spiritual warfare; the blood of Abel cried to God against Cain his wicked brother; Genesis 4, the blood of lamb withstood the angel of death that was assigned against Egyptian first born; Exodus 12, the blood of Naboth hunt after king Ahab and family for revenge; 1 kings 21:19, 2 kings 9:26.

Think also about the blood of Jesus that speaks better things more that the blood of Abel; Hebrew 12:22-24.

Anytime you see the mark or stain of blood on your door post or at the entrance of your door, there is danger or fear of evil monitors. Though all these things is not to make you afraid, but to be battle ready against spiritual wickedness; you will surely win as you fight according to the instructions in this book for spiritual warfare.

8. WHEN YOU ALWAYS HEAR MOVEMENTS IN THE CEILING ESPECIALLY AT NIGHT.

Often times people thought that it is rat that is always running up and down in their ceiling, well, some times they may be right, but they are not always right. Evil monitors hides almost everywhere within their reach to carry out their wicked acts.

They hide inside ceiling, but watching to control the destiny of their victims. But, a complete turn to Jesus in repentance, and a serious fight against them with a well arranged weapon of spiritual warfare will push them out and deliver their victims forever.

Think about that; evil watchers or monitors are real, but the power of prayer in the name of Jesus puts them to flight just as you made mention of the name of Jesus Christ. Give Jesus a chance to help you out.

9. WHEN YOU START HEARING UNSEEN FOOT STEPS AROUND YOU.

When the devil is up against someone everything will fall apart. The devil does not spare or select where to tread whenever he gain access into a soul, he tries to destroy and dominate everything his hands could catch up with..

Imagine hearing an unseen sound of someone's foot steps, whether in the day or night, it is enough to make someone run when he is not seeing the person pursuing him; madness, the evil monitor is dangerous, and not a respecter of anybody.

10. WHEN YOU EAT OR HAVE SEX IN THE DREAM.

Having sex or eating in the dream is one of the means that the devil is using to cage people or trap them for manipulation according to his desires. As I said earlier, the devil cannot come and possess or put yoke on you until you open up a way for him through sin or an immoral act.

Sin is the power darkness has over men; without sin the devil cannot enter or destroy your life or your business. So you have to be careful what you do or how you conduct yourself, he is watching with an evil eye, and very ready to destroy.

Though you may not be able to control what happens in the dream, but your activities and behaviors in the day contributes a higher percentage to what you dream; so, be careful and walk in the light of the word of God for onward control of the Spirit of grace in all your affairs.

PRAYER

1.Father I bless your name because you loves me so much, and you have already given your Son Jesus for my deliverance before now.

2. I acknowledge the power in your spoken words, and your readiness to deliver me as I pray; I will by no doubt go for my deliverance immediately in Jesus name.

3. I dedicate my life to seeking your face, and living the life of righteousness, from now onward I will live for you O Lord in Jesus name

4. Father I demand for the infilling of your Spirit, I cannot do it all alone; therefore Lord, help me and fill me now with sings of speaking in other tongues in Jesus name.

5. I cover my decision with the blood of Jesus, and I command blindness on every monitoring eyes hovering over my life in Jesus mighty name.

CHAPTER FOUR

WHAT SHALL WE DO NOW

Acts 16 :25-31; but at mid night Paul and Silas were praying and singing hymns to God, and the prisoners were listening to them. Suddenly there was a great earth quake, so that the foundation of the prison were shaken; and immediately all the doors were opened and everyone's chain were loosed.

And the keeper of the prison, awaken from sleep and seeing the prison door open, supposing the prisoners had fled, drew his sword and was about to kill himself.

But Paul called with a laud voice saying; do yourself no harm for we are all here. Then he called for a light, ran in, fall down trembling before Paul and

Silas. And he brought them out and sais, sirs, what must I do to be saved? So they said, believe on the Lord Jesus Christ, and you will be saved, you and your house hold.

I know already that there is fear in the heart of someone over the menace of evil monitors. Yes, their wickedness is enough to male a mortal man to be afraid, or ever run away from his house or country or state.

But the solution is not running away from your place or country, but to look inward, and discover the saving grace in the Lord Jesus Christ, which was made available to every human, especially them that believe in His name..

So according to the jailer; what must I do to be saved should be the best question at this point. What to do is a must, and must be done quickly because the evil watcher or monitor is determined to steal, kill and destroy without any delay.

So, if you love yourself, and you are ready to be delivered, there is a way out; and the way as was even disclosed to the Philippians jailer is; believe on the Lord Jesus Christ and you will be saved.

So, now come the true and sincere question for the hour "what must I do to be saved"?

The question about salvation and deliverance is for someone and anyone that would want to see better days in life; this is because some serious steps must be taken to stop evil before things grow worst.

John3:14; and as Moses lifted up the serpent in the wilderness, even so must the son of man be lifted up, that whoever believes in Him should not perish but have everlasting life.

Believing in Jesus Christ is a high way for deliverance from the menace of the evil monitors, and it has to be followed up with some certain steps to ensure efficiency and profitability. The steps are as follows:

1.DECISION

Deuteronomy 30:19-20; I call heaven and earth as witnesses today against you, that I have set before you life and death, blessing and cursing, therefore choose life, that both you and your descendants may live; that you may love the Lord your God, that you may obey His voice, and that you may cling to Him, for He is your life and the length of your days; and that you may dwell in the land which the Lord your God swore to your fathers, to Abraham, Isaac, and Jacob, to give them.

The danger of the evil monitors are too much and too deadly that no one would like to manage it for a season, it frustrate lives, and even cause death entirely. So, turning against it needs a quick and quality decision.

This is a decision that cannot be hindered by any circumstances. It will put fire in your bone to stop at nothing until you receive your deliverance, and recover all your wasted glories.

Decision brings determinations, which at a long run effect your destiny; it is decision that interprets what you will be in life or what your life will look like; either great or otherwise.

Zechariah 3:6-7; then the Angel of the Lord admonished Joshua saying, thus says the Lord of Hosts; if you will walk in my ways, and if you will keep my commands, then you shall also judge My house, and likewise have charge of my courts. I will give you places to walk among these who stand here.

If you can decide today, you will go ahead to obey all His commands that will lead to your deliverance, and quality life, and you will stand in the same place with God's chosen; people that inherits His benefit in this life.

It is good to be a Christian; answer Christian names, but it is of more benefit to be among those believers who have made up their minds to search and obey the word of God; those sets are qualified for the blessed hope.

Decision makes you to separate your self from multitudes; people that are not careful about what God says, and how to keep his commands. This separated life will make the power and attention of

God to be on your life, and God will manifest His beauty and glory in everything you do.

Daniel 1:8; but Daniel purposed in his heart that he would not defile himself with the portion of the king's delicacies, nor with the wine which he drank; ...

Daniel decided, and he was distinguished and delivered by God amongst all others in the land, and that decision promoted him to the level of divine manifestation for outstanding testimony that cannot be forgotten till this day.

Can you summon courage to decide to look for freedom from evils that are gathered to destroy your life? It will pay you off with some glorious blessings that will make your life shine in the near future, just take decision, it pays.

2. CONVERSION

PSALM19:7; the law of the Lord is perfect, converting the soul; the testimony of the Lord is sure, making wise the simple.

Conversion is talking about a change, you need to change your course of life, and turn to pleasing God in all your ways; putting the laws of God into consideration in whatever you do.

To converting to obey the laws of God will bring you to a realm where God is in charge, where all things are made possible by the Spirit of God. In this life, things are made possible by the Spirit of God

When you get converted to Jesus, the Spirit of God will take over your life, and everything that concerns you, He will fight for you, and lead you in all your ways, and you will have good success to the praise of His name.

But if you have not been converted to Him, if you are still living your life as you like without considering the laws of God, you will just be empty and void of the blessings of God.

The ability to make wealth or be prosperous is traceable to the knowledge and obedience of the word of God. It is God that gives life and also power to make wealth. So think inward, think Jesus

Christ; there is no other name that can gain us salvation except through the name of Jesus Christ.

Acts 4:10 and 12; let it be know to you all, and to all the people of Israel, that by the name of Jesus Christ of Nazareth, whom you crucified, whom God raised from the death, by Him this man stands here whole. Nor is there salvation in any other, for there is no other name under heaven given among men by which we must be saved.

If you can turn to Jesus Christ, and accept Him now, you will be saved, and be delivered as you turn to fight powers that are fighting you. But without Jesus in your life, you will not have spiritual back up for a successful spiritual warfare that will set you free from the demonic eye that is monitoring your life affairs, and lift you to the level of praise that God has prepared for you.

Until you turn to Jesus, nothing happens. Some people out of ignorant are pursuing deliverance through a wrong channel, some are just living by the mercy of God, they don't know what to do so that they can be saved; but God is merciful and gracious, He has prepared a high way for deliverance, to as many that will turn in obedient to the laws and commands of God to be delivered.

Acts 17:30; truly, these times of ignorant God overlooked, but now commanded all men everywhere to repent.

3. CONSECRATION

Consecration means to set apart or to keep holy. God is holy, and He does not associate with anything unclean or unholy. If you want to receive anything from God or you want to associate with Him so as to receive His blessings; you must be ready to consecrate yourself, keep yourself holy so that His Spirit can access your life for divine intervention.

The children of Israel under the leadership of Joshua was highly in need of God's intervention on their affairs, they needed to continue their journey to the promise land, but this time it was to cross the river Jordan.

Crossing the river Jordan where there was no bridge required divine interventions; miracles. It was only God that can save at a time like this, and all eyes was on God to do as he did while they were at the bank of the red sea, they were all waiting.

And Joshua came up with a wise decision according to the word of God, to help them pave way for the Spirit of God to manifest in their midst as before; so he asked them to separate themselves for God to manifest and give them what they were looking for.

Joshua3:5; and Joshua said to the people, sanctify yourselves, for tomorrow the Lord will do wonders among you.

This sanctification means to put away sins and start living life of holiness unto the Lord everyday. That holy living will attract the Spirit of God into your life to begin to process and to do what only God can do in your life.

John 15 :4-5; abide in Me and I in you, as the branch cannot bear fruit of itself, unless it abides in the vine, neither can you unless you abide in Me.

I am the vine, you are the branches, he who abides in Me, and I in him, bears much fruits, for without Me you can do nothing.

You need to be delivered, yes, you will be delivered, but you need to abide in Jesus Christ. Abiding in Jesus means following Him with every sincerity, obeying His words, and commands, and without fail living a life of righteousness. As you seriously go into this, the Spirit of God will take over you, and everything that concerns you, to guide and to protect for onward glorifications in all things.

4.COMMITMENT.

John13:17; if you know these things, blessed are you if you do them.

Procrastination or postponement is a trick of the devil to lengthen or extend the period of your slavery, so anything you want to do, do it fast. Until you get yourself committed into a thing it remains a dream or an idea not explored, and it will not yield any fruit.

There is no doubt about your divine support, it is the earnest desire of the Almighty to grant unto you whatever you desire or cry for. He said , "ask and it shall be given to you".

Besides, God has chosen you and would want you to prosper in whatever you do; His words are not word of men, they are true and forever settled in heaven that men will know that there is a God in heaven who care for the salvation and fruitfulness of His people.

John15:16; you did not choose Me, but I chose you and have appointed you that you should go and bear fruit, and that your fruit should remain, that whatever you ask the Father in My name, He may give you.

You are not serious, you are not yet ready for deliverance, sincerely you want to die in the hand of your enemy when you are not committed to your deliverance or fight that will set you free.

What are you waiting for? The word of God had announced your support since the day began, and Angels of God are all ready waiting for you to kick off so that they can back you up and restore your freedom and glory back to you.

Listen; victory is not by man power though, but by the Spirit of the Living God, and the Spirit of God, His ministering Spirits are set according to biblical order to help you, why wasting time? Get committed to the assignment and have your crown of victory on your heady for the power belongs to God.

PRAYER

1. Father I thank you for opening my inner eyes to see heavenly support for my deliverance, I will move forward in Jesus name.

2. I will not let the devil win the battle; neither will I compromise with sin or anything that will delay my deliverance in Jesus name.

3. I resist any power manipulating my mind to still considering a day in the cage of my enemy in Jesus name.

4. I revolt today to their tricks, I move forward to my onward deliverance and recovery of my destiny in Jesus name.

5. I stand and resist every weakness and every influence of powers of darkness that will make me neglect prayers or forget my weapons of spiritual warfare as I go into the battle in Jesus name.

CHAPTER FIVE

GET READY FOR SPIRITUAL WARFARE

Getting read for a fight or war is getting to acquire weapons and alliance, supports that make you fit or fortified to fight and win the battle. Even in physical war or fight, preparation is often more important than going into the fight proper.

If you are not prepared, going in for a fight or war will just be as good as committing suicide; you don't with your right senses go into a battle or war without a good preparation, it is a death sentence, it is foolishness.

Everything spiritual has its way and directions written and directed in the scripture. If you follow biblical standard and directions as you go into spiritual warfare or walk, you must come out victorious.

This is because the scripture is the word of God, it is supernaturally backed up, and cannot fail; it stands forever fortified by God Himself. So follow the scriptural order as you go into battle, you will never stumble or fail.

2 Corinthians 10:3-6; for though we walk in the flesh, we do not war according to the flesh. For the weapons of our warfare are not carnal but mighty in God for pulling down strongholds,

Casting down arguments and every high thing that exalts itself against the knowledge of God, bringing every thought into captivity to the obedience of Christ, and being ready to punish every disobedience when your obedience is fulfilled.

The scripture above cleared ground on the questions to know the type of battle you are getting ready to fight. Knowledge of the type of battle your are about to fight will go a long way to make you know who fights, and the type of preparations that will be fitting for the battle.

According to the scripture or bible quotation above, though we walk in the flesh; we live or walk about in the flesh as human beings, but we don't war or fight according to the system or style of the fleshly or physical fight or warfare of guns and pistols.

But the weapons we use in fighting are such that were made strong by God, which can pull down strongholds. There are strong holds that were established spiritually in the heavenly places.

Ephesians 6:12; for we do not wrestle against flesh and blood, but against principalities, against powers, against the rulers of darkness of this age, against spiritual hosts of wickedness in the heavenly places.

They are spiritual beings, and must be confronted with spiritual weapons if winning the battle is anything to think about. You don't fight spirits with clubs, Guns or by boxing with your fists, no, it is an error, you need spiritual weapons to go so that you can win the battle and recover all your stolen virtues.

Ephesians 6:10; finally, my brethren, be strong in the Lord and in the power of His might. Put on the whole armors of God, that you may be able to stand against the wiles of the devil.

So, Spiritual weapons that must be ready and sure within your reach are as follows:

1.HELMET OF SALVATION

If you go into a battle that will swallow your head, or a war that will blow off your head, then crown or no crown is useless. As a good warrior, you must make sure that your head is well covered before stepping into the battle field. This is very important because the first target of your enemies is your head, if they blow off your head then the battle is over, they have won.

Therefore take the helmet of salvation; Ephesians 6:17, this must be the number one weapon and armor you must endeavor to acquire before talking about going for spiritual warfare.

The process of getting and putting on your helmet of salvation is by accepting the Lord Jesus Christ as your Lord and Savior. This means, making Jesus the owner and controller of your life. And at this point His words must be the determinant factors for your life, in acts or behaviors.

Colossians 3:16-17; let the word of Christ dwell in you richly in all wisdom, teaching and admonishing one another in psalms and hymns and spiritual songs, singing with grace in your hearts to the Lord. And whatever in the word or deed, do all in the name of the Lord Jesus, giving thanks to God the Father through Him.

As the word of Christ dwell in you richly, it will begin to manifest in your speech and in your action, thus controlling your life into the light of God that brings deliverance

John 8:12; then Jesus spoke to them again saying; I am the light of the world. He who follows Me shall not walk in darkness, but have the light of life.

It is the light of Jesus that brings salvation, and deliverance from all darkness, and every ill that follow darkness, including evil monitors. So, put that in your store house, and then continue your preparations.

2. RIGHTEOUSNESS

Knowledge of the laws of God will make a determined heart to be careful how he behaves in all of his conducts. God knew what will befall or face Joshua when He instructed His to meditate on the laws of God, and be careful not to turn to the right or left.

As you add righteous living to your store house in preparation for your spiritual warfare, you will be exalted into the level of the exalted throne of Jesus, and you will be far above principality and powers, and all spiritual wickedness.

Proverbs 14:34; righteousness exalts a nation but sin is a reproach to any people.

As you go over to battle against your enemies, beware, don't touch or associate with anything unclean, remain in the land and teachings of your God, and He will grant your heart desires at the appointed time which is now.

3. THE SWORD OF THE SPIRIT

The sword of the spirit is the word of God. In this spiritual battle, you will need the sword of the spirit to spiritually cut into pieces every obstacle on your way, and to cut off the head of your enemy as God brings them down in your presence.

Hebrew4:12; for the word of God is living and powerful, and sharper than any two edged sword, piercing even to the division of soul and spirit, and of joint and marrows, and is a discerner of the thought and intent of the heart.

2 Corinthians 10:5;..... bringing every thought into captivity to the obedience of Christ.

The sword of the spirit will discern your thoughts and the intents of your heart, and will bring it into the obedience of Christ. If your thought is not in obedience of Christ, you will not have a divine back up for effectual spiritual warfare.

But as you stock your mind full with the sword of the spirit, you will be able to cut off every negative thought that is going against the order and commands of Christ; the victory, and deliverance you are looking for can only be gotten or achieved in the name of Jesus Christ.

So borrow from Joshua the son of Nun the leader of the children of Israel in reading and meditating in the word of God daily so that your way will be prosperous, and you will have good success as recommended.

4.THE NAME OF JESUS

Many Christians are not well informed, they claim to be Christ's but His name is very far from their mouth. This is because the word of Christ is not dwelling in there heart richly, so they hardly remember to call out or to call on the name whenever they are in danger or faced with some unexpectedness.

There is something of note, highly important, "we are saved by the grace that is in Jesus Christ, you cannot come to God or get blessings or answer to your request unless you come through Jesus Christ; neither can you receive divine or angelic assistance for anything whatever unless you approach heaven or call out the name of Jesus Christ".

On that note, you must have the name of Jesus registered in your subconscious mind, so you will always call out on Him as occasion demands for onwards help and deliverance.

God is the most supreme, and the only one that can save or deliver, but you can only access the throne of God through prayers in the name of Jesus otherwise your enemy will take you for a prey.

John14:6; Jesus said to them; I am the way, the truth, and the life. No one comes to the Father except through Me.

5.FAITH

By faith we talk about believing in God and all His words. God is Spirit, and whoever that is coming to

Him must believe that He exist though you are not seeing Him.

Though you are not seeing God, and you have not seeing Him once, but testimonies about Him proves that He exist, and He is a rewarder of people that seeks His ways and promises.

Father Abraham did not see Him even once, but he believed His words of promises, and God grant to him a divine approval; he was blessed even at his old age.

Yes God is Spirit, and He uses His Angels as ministering Spirits; as you have faith in Him and His spoken words, His Angels will work in your life and your affairs, and will do wonders to your amazement. But before you will please God, and move Him to action to the point of saving you, you must have faith.

Hebrew 11:6; but without faith it is impossible to please Him, for he who comes to God must believe that He is, and that He is a rewarder of those who diligently seek Him.

By faith many men in the olden time received deliverance in divers ways; the three Hebrew boys where saved from the burning furnace; Daniel 3:19-25, and Daniel was not eaten by lions though they threw him into the den; Daniel 6:10-23,

The hand and power of God that delivers are still very active today, and will deliver you; but you have to remove doubt and put on the armor and weapon of faith.

Faith is a shield; with faith you can quench every fiery dart the enemy might throw against you, but without faith you will be going to the battle alone; without the support of the Spirit of God.

The hands of God is upon you now that you have given your life to Jesus; but you have to believe that He is able to deliver you and restore all your wasted blessings; by this He will know that your trust is upon Him, then He will be moved to take action in your favor.

When you have faith on God, He will bring His promises over your life to manifestation, and the wounds and destructive effect of the agents of darkness in your life will be a forgotten issue.

6.THE BLOOD OF JESUS CHRIST

The blood of Jesus is both the weapon and armor for spiritual warfare. The blood of Jesus can be used for defensive and offensive; you can cover yourself with the blood of Jesus as a protective covering, and you can also use the blood of Jesus to destabilize the alliance of the evil one against your life and purpose.

But when you are ignorance of all these things, you will neglect putting it in your stock as you get ready for spiritual warfare. If you know these tricks, you will ever have the blood of Jesus ready in your mouth for protections and for a weapon to attack your adversaries.

Revelation 12:11; and they overcame him by the blood of the Lamb and by the word of their testimony.....

The qualification you have to stand against Satan is because the blood of Jesus was shed on the cross for your sake and for the remission of your sins. So, whenever Satan or the devil rises up to harass you or to oppose your freedom, you will lift the weapon of the blood for your protection, and a certificate of your salvation.

It is like telling the devil that you don't have anything with him again; that the blood has been shed for the payment of whatever debt you owe him in the past because of sin; and if the devil sees the blood, he will be weak and unable to harm or attack you further.

So be wise and arm yourself with the blood of Jesus Christ always, the devil will not be able to come near you or harm you.

7.PRAISES

It is very sad to note that many Christians do not have enough word and songs of praise and worship, they are always rushing to tell God their pains and troubles immediately they entered their prayer room; it is an error; a mistake.

Is it a surprise to you that God don't eat meat or milk, His delight is in the praises of His people. If you praise God, He will appear and stand by you in any situation, either to bless you or to fight your enemy.

In 2 Chronicles 20; the Lord directed King Jehoshaphat not to go against their enemies with carnal weapons of guns and clubs, but to stand before them and praise His holy name.

Obedient to this single instruction gave them victory against their oppressors. While they were singing, God came down and put confusion in the midst of their enemies, and they began to kill themselves while the king and the whole Israel were just watching. Can you see God in action, saving His name, and delivering His people?

Praise is appropriate, it is right to praise the Lord; praise is lovely, you will be happy as you praise Him in the beauty of holiness; try praises as weapon of spiritual warfare, and you will ever go again to confront your enemy with praises to God as victory will be your portion.

PRAYER

1.Father I surrender my life to you, I will forever cherish your salvation all the days of my life in Jesus name.

2. I rededicate my life and my service to you O Lord, fill me with your power in Jesus name.

3. I wear my spiritual weapons with my helmet of salvation, I will never operate in the camp of the devil in Jesus name.

4. I now awake to righteousness, and I go by the power of the Holy Spirit to possess my possessions in Jesus name.

5. Thank you father for saving me and making me a vessel of honor, and an instrument for deliverance in Jesus name.

CHAPTER SIX

WHO IS QUALIFIED TO FIGHT

Spiritual warfare is not a battle for everybody; it is a fight against spiritual wickedness in the high places. Human being can't fight spirits, before you fight spiritual battle you must be careful to make sure that you meet up to the standard for spiritual warfare.

It is only God that can save man when it comes to fighting spiritual wars, and without God or the Spirit of God in you, you are not good to go into battle, spirits fights spirits.

So for you to go into spiritual warfare, you must meet up with the following requirements:

1.YOU MUST BE BORN AGAIN

John3:3; Jesus answered and said unto him, most assuredly, I say to you, unless one is born, again, he cannot see the kingdom of God.

To be born again is a high point that must be made before you start talking about going to fight spiritual warfare. And to be born again you need Jesus into your life, accept Him as your savior and Lord so that you will be accepted by God.

It is only God that can save through Jesus Christ, without that you are not qualified to fight the battle.

John14:6; Jesus said to him, I am the way, the truth, and the life, no one comes to the Father except through Me.

You need Jesus in your life, already you are into errors of sins, and it will take the entrance of Jesus into your heart before you will be considered by God for forgiveness, and onward to the presence of God before deliverance from the cage of the devil or evil monitors.

As you accept the Lord Jesus as your Lord and Savior, He will save you. The process of your salvation includes the entrance of His Spirit into your life; His Spirit will lead you to all truth and destroy every foundation of errors in your life thereby set you free completely from darkness and all their works.

2. MAINTAIN YOUR SANCTIFICATION

Romans 3:23; for all have sinned and fall short of the glory of God.

It was sin that made man to fall short of the glory of God; in the beginning it was not so. God created man with every deposit of His power and glory, but the fall of man made him dead and empty before God.

The man full of the glory of God cannot be sick, neither can any creature harass him. Every thing was going as God planned because the Spirit of God was with the obedient and dedicated man until sin do them part.

Accepting Jesus is reconciling to God so He can restore His Spirit and glory back as in the beginning. This will mean that His Spirit will take over you and all your affairs, and you will be full of His glory again as of in the beginning.

So, when this is done, you must be very careful to maintain your sanctification; remain holy unto the Lord. Your holy living will pronounce your deliverance so loud that it cannot be resisted.

1 Thessalonians 4:3-4; for this is the will of God, your sanctification; that you should abstain from sexual immorality; that each of you should know how to possess his own vessel in sanctification and honor.

3. LET THE WORD OF GOD DWELL IN YOU RICHLY

Colossians 3:16-17; let the word of Christ dwell in you richly in all wisdom, teaching and admonishing one another in psalms and hymns and spiritual songs, singing with grace in your hearts to the Lord.

And whatever you do in word or deed, do all in the name of the Lord Jesus, giving thanks to God the Father through Him.

The word of God is powerful, the word of the Lord is creative, it gives life to the lifeless, and makes things that are not to come into being. As you allow the word of God dwell in you richly through continuous and serious studies, your life will experience a recreation, things will turn around for your good.

The word of God in your life will introduce the light of God which stand to chase away and resist darkness continually in your life; and you will ever be delivered from errors and mistake that rue men into darkness and captivity.

Matthew 22:29; Jesus answered and said to them, "You are mistaken not knowing the scripture nor the power of God".

The word of God delivers from errors, and you know, it is errors or mistakes that leads to slavery or bondage in the hand of the devil; it is mistakes that made evil monitors to penetrate into your life and destroy your glory.

So, as you stock up your heart with the word of God, you will be made wise, you will know what and how to walk in other to avoid sins and shortness of the glory of God.

Study to fill your heart with the word of God, and you will prosper, and you will have good success.

4. BE FILLED WITH THE HOLY SPIRIT

Ephesians 1:11-13; in Him also we have obtained an inheritance, being predestined according to the purpose of Him who works all things according to the counsel of His will, that we who first trusted in Christ should be to the praise of His glory.

In Him you also trusted, after you heard the word of truth, the gospel of your salvation; in whom having believed, you were sealed with the Holy Spirit of promise.

The Holy Spirit was given to all believers in Jesus Christ for a seal; the gift of the Holy Spirit is for all so long as you are in the number of the chosen of God; He is a free gift to all. So if you don't have Him in your life, you got to rise up and ask the Father to anoint you with the Holy Spirit of promise, it is your right.

Holy Spirit will fill you with wisdom amongst other things, and you will know what to do at every point of your walk with the Father in this life. He will deliver you from mistakes, and make your deliverance to be permanent.

1 John2:20; but you have an anointing from the Holy one, and you know all things.

Be filled with the Holy Spirit, and you will neither be weak or barren in the land of your deliverance, neither will you suffer miscarriage on the way in Jesus mighty name.

PRAYER

1.Father I thank you for opening my eyes to all these things, I will abide by them in Jesus name.

2. I will forever dedicate my life to you O Lord, to serve and worship you all the days of my life in Jesus name.

3. Forgive me Lord of all my past sins, I will never give the devil a chance in my life, to put me into captivity again in Jesus name.

4. As I begin to pray Lord, let you glory cover me, and let all my stolen virtues begin to flow back to me in Jesus name.

5. I open my heart to the Holy Spirit, Fill me now sweet Holy Spirit, and make me an instrument of righteousness in Jesus name.

CHAPTER SEVEN

FIGHTING THE BATTLE

Jeremiah 50:33; thus says the Lord of hosts; *" The children of Israel were oppressed, along with the children of Judah; and who took them captive have held them fast; they have refused to let them go.*

Their Redeemer is strong; the Lord of hosts is His name. He will thoroughly plead their case, that He may give rest to the land, and disquiet the inhabitant of Babylon.

Something is about to happen here! Fight! Fire is burning on the mountain, Satan and all his allies must perish or release their captive for the Lord has risen to deliver Zion.

In this fight, there is no mercy because the devil has over stayed his welcome, he has eaten what that was meant for the sons of God, he has matched were he is not allowed to match.

The weapons of our warfare are not carnal but mighty in God, so we are going to consult God for this fight for we belong to Him, we are the children of His pasture; He is our Shepherd.

We are going to raise the sword of battle in prayer; prayer is the access code to the throne of heaven; when we pray, when we access heaven the unshakable will shake; let's go to battle.

Jeremiah 50:35-37; a sword is against the Chaldeans, says the Lord, against the inhabitant of Babylon, and against her princes, and her wise men. A sword is against the soothsayers, and they will be fools, a sword is against the mighty men, and they will be dismayed.

A sword is against their horses, against their chariots, and against all the mixed peoples who are in her midst, and they will become like women. A sword is against her treasures, and they will be robbed.

The hand of the Almighty will do all these things as you stand up to pray; remember, you are a weapon in the hand of the Almighty God.

Jeremiah 51:20; you are my battle axe and weapons of war. For with you I will break the nations in pieces; and with you I will destroy kingdoms.

At this point we will be discussing a crucial point of this chapter, and that is prayers.

PRAYERS

For a believer to stand out victorious in the battle of life with their complete armors, there must be constant and earnest administration of prayers. It is through prayer that the believers' spiritual armor will be first put on, and then made effective; without effective prayers, our enemies will take us to be joking or playing

It is through prayers of faith that believers put on their weapons and armors for spiritual warfare, and also put them into use for the pulling down of strong holds and spiritual wickedness in high places; delivering all those that were held captive in the prison room of the devils and his agents.

Believers were implored to pray and watch unto that continuously; this means that, if you have learnt to pray, make sure you are seriously praying always. Emphasis on continuous prayers was repeatedly spoken by our Lord and Savior Jesus Christ because He knows that the devil is mad against God's creatures, so believers should arise and give him a fight in the name of Jesus.

Prayer is a strong weapon in the hand of believers for spiritual warfare, and it was approved by God Himself; hence He said "You are my battle axe and my weapon of war". As you pray, God will by His Spirit be taking over the territories of the devil.

But there is need to watch while praying, asking some sincere questions that would help to make our prayers more effective. And such question includes what spiritual weapons that could be used for better response and faster result as we pray?

Just as you should still remember that there are different weapons for spiritual warfare, like; the blood of Jesus, the name of Jesus, the word of God, and praises. Those weapons were powerfully used by believers in the ancient time, and they did exploits. So you should discern the weapon to put into use for immediate result as you pray.

BRANCHES OF PRAYERS

Ephesians 6:18; and pray in the spirit on all occasions with all kinds of prayers and requests. With this in mind, be alert and always keep on praying for all the saints (niv)

Knowledge of different kind of prayers will help a prayer warrior to get to his destination accurately and on time. As you can see, there are kinds of prayers, and if you know this and you are using it, it will be a bunch of blessings to you as it helps you achieve your goals easily.

Let's look at few types before we go further;

1.PRAYER OF WORSHIP .

Proverbs 10:14; wise people store up knowledge, but the mouth of the foolish is near to destruction.

Now, because of ignorant and lack of the word, some people find it difficult to worship God, they would always like to ask or make request for their selfish desires.

That is an error. Our God is worthy of our worship; when we worship, we bring down the present of God to act on our request, but when we don't care about the present of God, and we are just praying because we are in need, it will be a mistake because without the presence of God in your prayers, all you are doing is noise making; no results, so be careful on that and do the necessaries.

2. PRAYER OF CONFESSION

No matter who you are, in as much as you are still human, you cannot deny sin or mistakes. So in order not to risk your prayers, you need to maintain a clean plate before going to ask for some more.

When you neglect prayer of confessions, you are like saying that you don't care whether your prayers are answered or not, and prayers not answered is a waste of time, and no body will chose to waste his time on that; so be careful as you go into your prayers.

3. PRAYER OF THANKGIVING

Philippians 4:6;.....with thanksgiving, let all your request be made known to God.

Our Lord Jesus commended a leper that came back to thank Him after discovering that he was made clean, and he also asked of the remaining nine.

Literary, it is very wrong to approach the king or even a person who has done something good for you without thanks, even if you are not in need of more.

If you cannot thank, you will be assumed to either be foolish or wicked, and you don't deserve further favor or goodness, so beware whenever you go to God in prayers, firstly give Him thanks for choosing you and for the privilege to pray, also for answer to your previous requests.

4. PRAYER OF SUPPLICATION OR PETITION

At this point, you are set to demand or request what you desire. At this junction you must be specific, and with a clear language. Don't ask what you don't need or out of foolishness, be wise.

It is not a wonder that our heavenly Father knows what we need even before we open our mouth to ask; yes He knows as He is all knowing God, but when you come up with some bogus request without a good sense, He will take you as one that is not matured or serious. So, be warned.

OBSTACLES TO PRAYERS
1. TIREDNESS

Because of some daily activities we tend to be tired at the end of the day to continue our prayers in the night hour, but that is usually a device of the devil to hinder our blessings, and prolong our captivity.

But if your eyes are open to spiritual warfare, you will not consider weakness or tiredness when talking about prayer because the Spirit in you is the Spirit of power, as you turn to pray, He will increase your strength, and you will achieve your aim.

2. OVER EATING

It is good to eat so you can remain health, a sick person may not be able to pray or deliver his brother; but we must be careful while eating. Over eating has been a weapon or trick of the devil to lay Christians off their altars of prayer.

When you eat too much, your body will be too weak, and the next will be sleeping. The devil has used over eating to cast many wounded, so instead of over eating, why not fast or just eat a little, or even eat some hours before prayer time so that it will not stop you.

Remember, wisdom is the principal thing, as you are preparing for spiritual warfare, try to watch out tricks the devil is using to fight against your plans.

3. EXCESSIVE SLEEPING

Excessive sleeping is often caused by over eating or directly by demonic device. So to avoid that, you try to get yourself busy with something else before prayer time so yo u don't sleep off.

You can as well set your alarm clock to wake you up, in a general sense as a believer, you can ask the Holy Spirit to wake you up at a certain time, and He will not fail. So do every thing you know to overcome, and you will be glad you did.

4.RECURRING GUILTINESS

Lack of the knowledge of the word of God leads into many errors, and this includes, always feeling guilty any time you want to pray. You will be remembering sins you committed years back which you may have confessed, and probably forsaken.

That is the work of the devil to hinder your prayers. For Christ's sake, when you confess and forsake a particular sin, God has taken care of it, it is no more there, your are free indeed, the truth is that it can no more be associated with you again because the blood of Jesus has washed it away.

So tell the devil to get behind you, and continue your prayers.

5.DOUBT

Doubt is equally because of lack of faith, and lack of knowledge of the word of God. The bible says "Ask and it shall be given to you Matthew 7:7". "What ever you bind here on earth shall be bound in heaven, Matthew 18:18".

So why doubt, you have assurance of what you are asking even though it has not gotten to your hands, just wait with hope, it is on the way; don't doubt.

6. TOUGH CHALLENGES

The devil may tell you that God answered your previous request because that was a small case, but this present one is tough, and that God either cannot or may not answer easily.

Just tell the devil to get behind you; our God is the almighty, there is nothing He cannot do. As He turned water into wine by His power, the same way He made the dead to raise by the same His power; and He is able also to make that tough situation to bow down by the same His power, He has never changed.

7.LACK OF THE WORD OF GOD

Lack of the word of God in the life of a believer creates so much mistakes, it is the knowledge of the word of God that made us to be a good Christian. If you don't know the laws of God you will not even make effort to pursue or to do them.

But the knowledge of the word of God brings light and glory. It is when you know the word and work in the light of it that God will shower you with His glory, but outside that, your life will be filled with mistakes.

God respects His words, and He is always standing to perform His words whenever He hears it redirected to Him. But, when you don't know the word, how are you going to direct it to God in prayers.

The prayer that is wordless is a powerless prayer because it is the word of God commands powers. So, search and meditate on the word all the time, and also try as much as possible to always up load the word to God into your prayers, and even Satan cannot resist you whenever you are praying, it works faster.

HARMONY OF PRAYERS

Matthew 22:29; Jesus answered and say to them, you are mistaken not knowing the scriptures nor the power of God.

In the book of Matthew, the master taught us how or a pattern of prayer, and with a clear understanding, we need to see and know that He patterned it the way we can be attended to, and we should learn from Him as a perfect example.

But when we don't know the scriptures, we will be making some grievous mistakes; see the pattern once more:

Matthew 6:9; Our father in heaven, hallowed be your name, your kingdom come, you will be done on earth as it is in heaven, give us this day our daily bread. And forgive us our debts, as we forgave our debtors. And do not lead us into temptation, but deliver us from the evil one. For yours is the kingdom and power and the glory, forever, amen.

1.ADORATION OR WORSHIP

With worship or adoration you introduce yourself into the heavenly gate, and draw the attention of God towards your direction. Without God coming down to you or being attracted to your prayers first, everything you are saying is a waste of both time and efforts.

So, no matter the urgency of your needs, do the first thing first, and you will reap the results.

2. CONFESSION

Sin and mistakes dries the glory and oil of God in the life of men, and when you don't settle that before making your request, you will encounter so many troubles which include divine rejection.

But when you sweep away sins, you will have a portion in God for divine empowerment to recover all you may have wasted in the time past.

3. THANKSGIVING

While you are attending worship, confessions and thanks giving, your request and need are still there looking at you, but never mind, you are making a way for proper attention before God, and God knows even before now that you are in need of them.

So, never mind, do the first thing first, and you will never regret doing what is right. So, thank God for His goodness and kind dealings before going further to make any request.

4. SUPPLICATIONS

Supplications should be the last thing to present before God as you approach His throne of mercy. If you do otherwise, you may not receive divine attentions. You must be wise, and learn from the teachings of the master; it will help you.

The supplication may be to bind or to loose, it may be to decree or to declare; all put together, you must do that after attending to all those points above.

CHAPTER EIGHT

BINDING AND LOOSING

To bind in a broader sense means to restrict or to forbid a thing from taking place or a person from some areas or doing a particular thing which may cause harm. It also means to thwart satanic activities which at a large extent do not contribute to success or anything gainful.

In other way also, to loose means to untie things that was tied, or to release things that was restricted; to set free from bondage. However all these need higher power to either bind or loose.

This instructions or authority was given to believers in Christ Jesus, and you are included so long as you are born again; you can bind the devil, and also loose people that were oppressed by the devil, and the devil will not be able to harm you.

Matthew 16:19; and I will give you the keys of the kingdom of heaven, and whatever you bind on earth will be bound in heaven, and whatever you loose on earth will be loosed in heaven.

This authority or statement above was not for one person, neither was it for the old apostles, but for believers in Christ even if you are born again today.

So, now that you are in authority, you are expected to bind and loose for that is the will of God, and you have been given the authority. You can loose the power and glory of God over a place or thing, and you can also restrict or bind the devil over a person or thing as the case may be.

Remember, that is the will of God concerning you; so, get into doing it in obedient to the word of God and also to save and free yourself and your virtues; your blessings and glory that was trapped down by the devil.

PRAYERS FOR DELIVERANCE

PRAISES AND WORSHIP

CONFESSION OF SINS

PRAYER

1. Father I thank you for bringing me to this altar of power and deliverance, I will be delivered today in Jesus name.

2. I soak my spirit soul and body with the blood of Jesus, and I lift up the sword of the spirit against every hand writing registered against me in Jesus name.

3. I bring to nothing every evil assignment designed to destroy the purpose of God in my life in Jesus name.

4. All evil trees of non achievement, receive the axe of fire of God and be cut off forever in Jesus name.

5. I burst every evil spiritual vehicles assigned to carry me away from my destined greatness, and I set them on fire in Jesus name.

6. I release the sanitizing fire of God into the root of my life, to burn to ashes every deposit that frustrates my achievements in Jesus name.

7. I call back the glory of God back into my life, my life receive honor and dignity in Jesus name.

8. I break the monitoring mirror of witchcraft powers against my life in Jesus name.

9. I shall not be under the control of powers of darkness, for my life is hidden in God, I shall not be moved in Jesus name.

10. The blood of Jesus covers me as I believe in Jesus, and I will forever be saved from all devices of powers of darkness in Jesus name.

11. I cast into fire all materials of the agents of darkness, and I stop their inflow into my life in Jesus name.

12. I command every legal ground of my enemies into my life to be defiled with the blood of Jesus.

13. With the hammer of the word of God, I break every legal ground of my enemies to my life, and I stop their flows in Jesus name.

14. Spirit of the living God, move against every spirit moving and working against the fulfillment of my destiny in Jesus name.

15. I will be what the Lord my God want me to be, I refuse to walk into the cave of my enemy in Jesus name.

16. My name is written in the book of life and abounding success of God, I refuse to operate under the control of powers of darkness in Jesus name.

17. I am chosen by the almighty God to bear fruit, and I refuse to operate below my expectations in Jesus name.

18. Because the hands of God is upon my life, my life and destiny is well secured, I refuse to be exposed to the attack of my enemies in Jesus name.

19. O Lord, let my cry come unto you, and let the embargoes of my enemies over my life be lifted by the power of the Holy Ghost in Jesus name.

20. As the glory of God covered the people of Israel in the night and in the day, so shall the glory of God cover me from now to everlasting in Jesus name.

21. Multiple strong powers attached to my life to destroy my destiny, what are you waiting for be roasted by fire in Jesus name.

22. You evil pattern of unfruitfulness, the word of God is against you, break by fire in Jesus name.

23. I refuse to answer the name given to me by my enemies in Jesus name.

24. I enter into the circle of the purpose of the will of God to my life, and I refuse to be manipulated in Jesus name.

25. God has given His Angels charge over me, to keep and protect me wherever I go all the days of my life, I refuse not be manipulated by my enemies in Jesus name.

26. I exempt my glory from every manipulative image of evil monitors, and I hide under the protective power of God in Jesus name.

27. I commit my works and all my ways into the hands of God, and I refuse the results of my enemies over my ways and my works in Jesus name.

28. You evil I mage follow me, I command you to vanish into thin air in the name of Jesus.

29. I dominate every domonialing spirit assigned against my life; I conquer you today in Jesus name.

30. I stand in the most powerful name of Jesus, and I condemn every tongue of my enemy in every angle they are working against me in Jesus name.

31. I command every negative seal projected into the sun against my progress in Jesus name.

32. I stand pleading the blood of Jesus, and I destroy every decrees against my favor, and I command fire to devour every power projecting disfavor into my affairs in Jesus name.

33. O Lord reschedule my enemies to useless, and harmless assignments in Jesus name.

34. Let every good thing that is dead in my life life and begin to function excellently in Jesus name.

35. Let every evil of the enemy to monitor my movements and manipulate my expected results be shattered in Jesus name..

36. I put every seat of my enemies on fire, and I rise up by the power in the name of Jesus for excellence, honor and dignity in Jesus name.

37. I bind every spirit that is working against answers to my prayers, and I cast them into bottomless pit in Jesus name.

38. I loose every blessings released to me from the throne seat of heaven, and I command them to manifest into my life in Jesus name.

39. I will arise and shine, for the glory of the almighty God has risen upon my life, I shall not be ashamed any longer in Jesus name.

40. Glory of God that works out miraculous things, cover me and prosper my endeavors in Jesus name.

41. I command all satanic deposit into my life to be roasted by fire right now in Jesus name.

42. I remove my name from the book of untimely death and miscarriage of all types in Jesus name.

43. I remove and cast into fire every dirty hand of disfavor deposited into my life in Jesus name. and I declare my life favored in Jesus name.

44. I remove my name from the list of failures, and include my name in the list of successful men in Jesus name.

45. I refuse to be what my enemies want me to be, I agree and accept what the word of God says concerning me in Jesus name.

46. I revoke every conscious and unconscious covenant I have with agents of powers of darkness and the devils in Jesus name.

47. Healing power of Go overflow into my spirit, soul and mind now, and heal me of all wounds and manipulations in Jesus name.

48. I renounce every agreement I made or that was made un my behalf, consciously or unconsciously with evil altars and agents of darkness in Jesus name.

49. I disarm any power that has made agreement or covenant with the ground, water, wind and every power of darkness in the heavenly places in Jesus name.

50. I command all good things removed from my body by my enemies to be restored fully back in Jesus name.

51. Thank you Lord for delivering me in Jesus name

52. Thank you Lord for restoring my glory for fulfillments in Jesus name.

53. Thank you Lord for now am glad I am set free from the captivity of evil monitors in Jesus name.

54. I cover my deliverance and my recovery with the blood of Jesus Christ, and I demand that the Spirit of God keep guard over my life in Jesus name.

55. let my name become thunder and fire to my enemies, and whoever that will call me for evil manipulations in Jesus name.

CHAPTER NINE

CONCLUSION

To God be all the glory who led us through all the high way of the revelations of this book. I am glad and I believe that you have been blessed and delivered. Yes, if you have obediently followed my guardians which are according to biblical order, you are saved, and delivered.

Your enemy, the devil has lost the person he thought he has, and you are free in Jesus name.

But there are certain precautions I would like to let out to you, and it is my earnest desire that you also obediently keep to them even as you have done the rest of my advice in this book; the Lord keep on keeping you till His appearing, amen

HOW TO REMAIN SAFE AFTER DELIVERANCE

Proverbs 14:34; righteousness exalts a nation, but sin is a reproach to any people.

Sin is a reproach to any people; it was sin that made Adam and Eve to be driven from the garden, and a place of satisfaction that was made for them from the beginning.

Sin burns off the glory of God from the life of a man. If you would stay safe, and not be possessed back by more terrible demons, be far from sins. Sin kills; it makes a man enemy to his creator, and deprives him of his right from his heavenly inheritance; run away from sins.

1. SEARCH THE SCRIPTURE ALWAYS

Lack of the knowledge of the word of God makes a man to go into mistakes, and his life will be full of errors. If you know the word of God, your life will be full of light, and darkness, and agents of darkness will not have dominion over you.

Searching of the scripture was the order given by God to Joshua if he would like to prosper and have a good success in his leadership over the children of Israel. As you search the scriptures, the ways of God will be revealed to you, and the ability to walk in the light of His words will be received without stress.

2.HAVE FELLOWSHIP WITH BRETHREN

Hebrew 10:25; not forsaking the assembling of ourselves together, as is the manner of some, but exhorting one another, and so much the more as you see the Day approaching.

Gathering with your fellow brethren brings you closer to God and exposes you to a deep walk with the Holy Spirit. As you stay closer with other saints you will be learning from them, and you will be thirsty of the gifts that is in them.

As you continue with them, gradually you will be gifted according to the measure of your own faith also, and you will be delivered from the seduction of the world through lust.

3.KEEP TELLING OTHERS ABOUT JESUS CHRIST

Your testimony about Jesus will go a long way to save and give you a continuous deliverance from worldly characters. If you don't make yourself know as a believer, Satan will use style to draw closer to you.

Your testimony makes you a winner, and sustains your victory.

Revelation 12:11; and they overcome him by the blood of the Lamb and by the word of their testimony...

Go ahead to do all these command, and you will se yourself emerge victorious all the time in Jesus name. Remember, your faith in God and His written words are very important, believe also in me, for I have delivered to you the true counsel of the word of God.

PRAYER

. 1.I stand before God and you my brethren, and I declare today that belong to Jesus; Jesus is my

Lord and Savior, I will live the rest of my life for Him, I am no more for Satan again in Jesus name.

2. I dedicate my life to Jesus, and I renounce the devil and all his agents in the mighty name of Jesus.

3. I stand in the name of Jesus, and I command co fire and brim stone to fall in the camp of witchcrafts, and destroy everything I have with them.

4. I demolish every material of marine spirit in my custody, and I renounce their membership in the name of Jesus.

5. I cover my spirit soul and body with the blood of Jesus, and render useless every monitoring every monitoring eyes watching over my activities in Jesus name.

ABOUT THE BOOK

There are powers that manipulate the glorious deposit of God in the life of men, and blessings that are released to them from the throne seat of God. Those powers are functioning from spiritual wickedness in the high places.

They gain authority into men through the doors of sin in the lives of me, to steal, kill and destroy honor, dignity and excellence. They are real and they operate every where and on every body whether white or negro so long as there is trace of sin in the linage; it also try believer to make them err.

They have evil monitoring eyes to access and control men affairs to their evil wishes.

But there is power in God to destroy them, and deliver their victims. That is the purpose of this book.

This book talk extensively about evil monitoring eye, and what you can do to avoid their threats, stop heir propagations and deliver yourself, and also how to avoid being possessed again.

Are you a victim, do you feel the sign of their manipulation? Well, as you go through this book you will see by yourself, and also be able to deliver yourself by the power in the name of Jesus.

Save yourself from the evil one and your problems in life will be over. But there is high need of obedient to the orders and commands as directed in this book.

Happy deliverance and happy lasting freedom in Jesus name.

ABOUT THE AUTHOR

Apostle E N Livinus is a teacher and a dynamic preacher of the word of God, who by the power of the Holy Ghost exposes powers of darkness, and power of God unto deliverance to all those that was oppressed and are ready to come out from captivity.

In his books, he teaches how to know when you are oppressed, and what you must do to be delivered. Through this book many errors in deliverance prayers were exposed and corrected.

He also authored other books on deliverance and devotional prayers for your day by day devotional prayers, New Year, new months, and other deliverance processes that were used by oppressed peoples in the past.

He is the senior pastor of Divine Touch of God Praying Ministry, and he is married with Evangelist Nkeiruka Livinus, and God blessed them with children.

Printed in Great Britain
by Amazon